THE COMPLETE
POCKET GUIDE
TO
FLY FISHING

THE COMPLETE POCKET GUIDE TO FLY FISHING

by

Pat Fowler & Keith Breuker

Countrysport Press
Traverse City, Michigan

This edition of *The Complete Pocket Guide to Fly Fishing* was printed by Maury Boyd and Associates, Inc., Indianapolis, Indiana. The book was designed by Angela Saxon of Saxon Design, Traverse City, Michigan. The text is set in Berkeley Book.

© 1996 by Pat Fowler and Keith Breuker
Illustrations © 1996 by Jenny Leggett

First Edition
10 9 8 7 6 5 4 3 2 1

Published by Countrysport Press
1515 Cass Street, Traverse City, MI 49685

Printed in the United States of America

ISBN 0-924357-62-2

Cover Art by Steven Daiber

TO OUR WIVES

CONTENTS

INTRODUCTION

This may be the first book about fly fishing you're going to buy. If I know anything about this sport, it is probably not going to be your last. That, as you'll eventually discover, is one of the wonderful aspects of fly fishing for trout. It's been said that there have been more books written about trout fishing than about any other sport. And building a fly fishing library can bring lots of pleasure.

But for now, this is the only book you'll need. And I wish this book had been my first fly fishing book twenty-five years ago.

The Complete Pocket Guide to Fly Fishing takes the guesswork out of going fly fishing. Unlike some so-called guidebooks, this one doesn't try to overwhelm with unnecessary detail and minutia. And, best of all, it doesn't assume that you know the jargon. It covers all the basics of fly fishing in clear and precise language you can understand. And it has enough tips and tid-bits to make it a handy reference source even for the veteran angler.

How to pick an outfit, how to select the right leader (better yet—what a leader is!), how to attach the leader to the fly line, what fly to use and how to tie it to the leader, how to cast—it's all here and more. The authors, Pat Fowler and

Keith Breuker—veteran fly fishermen—even take you out onto the stream where they teach you to "read the water," that is, they teach you where the fish are most likely to be. And why. They also tell you *just enough* about trout behavior and what trout eat to make you dangerous. (There are literally hundreds of books on just those aspects of this sport.)

The authors have also included pictures of trout so you can identify what you catch. When I caught my first trout (pure luck) more than two decades ago I didn't even know what it was.

I'm impressed that the authors began this little book with a chapter on ethics. Most books that even bother to cover this important subject seem to save it for last, almost as an afterthought. We're making more fishermen but we're not making more trout streams. So a discussion about how we all get along on our irreplaceable trout waters is especially right—and right up front.

Having *The Complete Pocket Guide to Fly Fishing* is almost as good as having a real live guide. And it's designed so that it will fit in your vest.

This book tells you what you need to know to get started in fly fishing. The only thing it can't convey is the beauty of the places you're going to end up doing it, and the terrific people you'll meet along the way.

I hope I'm coming around the bend some sparkling spring evening just as your very first trout sips the Pale Morning Dun tied onto the end of your leader.

Best of luck.

—Jim Enger
Author, *The Incompleat Angler*

1 ETHICS

According to Gary Borger's video, "Where the Trout Are," the world's trout streams contain less than *one millionth of one percent* of the world's entire freshwater resources. And yet these rare and fragile ecosystems are continually burdened by residential land use, agricultural practices, and industrial development, to the extent that in less than one generation some of our most fertile rivers have lost their ability to produce native fish.

You can help reverse this trend by getting involved in a conservation organization such as Trout Unlimited or the Federation of Flyfishers whose members work collectively to ensure that our natural resources are protected and restored.

But just as important are the little things you can do individually to help preserve our sport:

- Always limit your catch, don't catch your limit.

- Always land your fish as quickly as possible. Don't play it to the point of exhaustion.

- When you can, release a fish without handling it. Using barbless hooks can help you release fish quickly.

- If you plan to eat a fish, kill it quickly. Never let fish suffer unnecessarily.

- Be sure to leave no rubbish behind when you're done fishing. Litter not only degrades habitat and dampens angling enjoyment, it also irritates property owners, who are less likely to allow access where anglers have abused the privilege.

- Respecting the rights of private property owners will make angling more pleasant for you and anglers who follow.

- Remember, many people pursue this sport to experience quiet and solitude.

- Don't disturb other anglers.

How you treat other anglers also contributes to your enjoyment. The golden rule ought to apply when passing or greeting another angler on the stream. Respecting the environment and each other's fishing experience will help everyone enjoy this wonderful sport of fly fishing.

2 GEARING UP

To begin the outfitting process you must first determine the fish you're seeking. That, in turn, determines the size of flies you'll be using, which then dictates the line and rod you'll need to cast those flies. In fly fishing, it's the weight of the line that casts the fly. Larger, more wind-resistant flies require heavier line and therefore a heavier rod. Most beginners start with a midrange 5-, 6-, or 7-weight line/rod combination. The following chart shows the approximate line/rod weights best suited for pursuing certain fish.

LINE/ROD WT.	SUGGESTED USES
1–2	panfish, small trout
3–5	medium trout, panfish
6–9	bass, steelhead, bonefish, larger trout, Atlantic salmon
10–12	stripers, small tarpon, bluefish, salmon, steelhead
13–15	tarpon, billfish, tuna

LINE SELECTION

Most trout anglers prefer 4- to 7-weight lines. Pike, bass, or light saltwater anglers using larger flies might prefer 7- to 10-weight outfits.

Advanced anglers using small flies for selective fish might use 1- to 3-weight lines for a delicate presentation. The 11 through 15 weights are big-game tackle. (For more information on choosing lines see chapter 3.)

ROD SELECTION

Next select a rod that matches your line. An inexpensive rod will get you started, but as you gain experience you'll appreciate the added performance and quality of higher-priced rods. Try some rods and decide for yourself if better performance justifies a higher asking price. In the end, always obtain the best quality your budget allows.

ROD ACTION

A fast-action rod flexes only near the tip when casting. A slow-action flexes its entire length.

Rod action is generally a matter of personal preference. You may want to first determine your rod-action preference, then limit your shopping to that type of rod. Your rod should cast easily, and the grip should feel comfortable in your hand.

Action types, from left to right: fast, medium, slow.

ANATOMY OF A FLY ROD

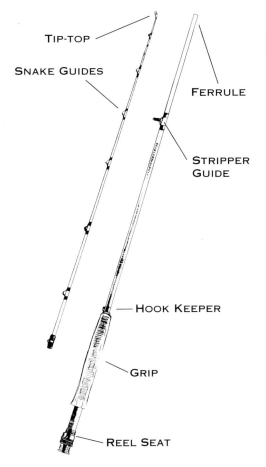

TIP-TOP

SNAKE GUIDES

FERRULE

STRIPPER GUIDE

HOOK KEEPER

GRIP

REEL SEAT

2

REEL SELECTION

Next choose a reel of sufficient line capacity for the line weight you'll be using. Allow for at least 20 yards of backing—more if you're angling for large fish. Backing provides not only extra line for hard-running fish, but a cushion for the line and a larger diameter base for winding the line. Matching the rod, line, and reel will give you a well-balanced outfit.

DRAG

Get the best drag system you can afford. Cost is usually an indicator of drag quality, but there is no better way to judge the quality of a reel's drag than actual fishing conditions. So don't be afraid to seek advice from experienced anglers when choosing a reel.

For smaller fish (up to a pound or so) a reel is just a place to store line you're not casting with. Landing larger fish that are strong enough to break your tippet, however, demands a smooth, adjustable drag system. The larger the fish, the more important the drag becomes. The drag adjustment should be easy to locate and should function smoothly.

SPOOLS

When comparing two reels with similar features, choose the one with the narrower spool. The narrower spool will wind line more evenly, making it less likely to tangle when the fish of a life-

ANATOMY OF A FLY REEL

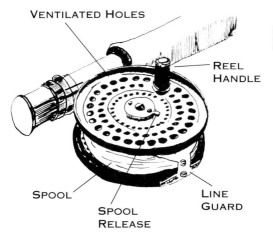

VENTILATED HOLES

REEL HANDLE

SPOOL

SPOOL RELEASE

LINE GUARD

time is rapidly peeling it from your reel. If you plan on fishing a variety of conditions, be sure to carry extra spools with different line weights for quick changes streamside.

DIRECT DRIVE

The most popular type of reel is the direct-drive, with the handle directly connected to the spool. This direct connection allows you to know exactly when you are gaining or losing line. One disadvantage of direct drive, however, is that the handle spins rapidly when a fish runs, posing a hazard to fingers. Anti-reverse reels solve the bruised finger problem and are especially use-ful for big-game fishing. But they are also more expensive and have more moving parts, increasing their potential for failure. Another reel option is the multiplier reel, which turns the spool more times than the handle so you can recover line quickly.

Reels should be cleaned and lubricated, per manufacturer's instructions, at least once a season, more frequently if needed.

WADERS

Bootfoot waders come with the boot attached directly to the wader fabric and are easier to get on and off than stockingfoot waders, which are used with separate boots that need to be laced over the wader. Some claim stockingfoot waders provide more comfort. But if you get bootfoot waders one-half-size larger, and then place a quality insole in the boot, there is little difference in comfort, and you'll be warmer in cold weather. Sorbethane is a good insole material because it does not absorb moisture and will not compress over time. Some insoles have arch support or heel lifts, like the kind you find in running shoes. Athletic-wear outlets, in fact, are good locations to shop for quality insoles.

While felt outer soles are essential for gripping the slippery algae-covered rocks found in many streams, lug soles will suffice for rivers that are mostly sand or mud. Also, lug soles do not pick up snow as felts do, and so provide better traction on land in wintery conditions.

Because creasing will reduce wader life, waders should be hung or rolled when not in use. If you roll your waders, dry them first. And always store your waders in a cool, dry place.

SUNGLASSES

A pair of polarized sunglasses is essential and will allow you to see fish obscured by surface glare. It will also ease eye strain on sunny days and provide eye protection from errant flies.

VESTS

When you evaluate a vest, wear it and check all the pockets for easy access. The zippers and other closures should work smoothly and be of good quality. A vest should be oversized to allow layered clothing underneath.

CLOTHING

For effective stalking, keep clothing colors drab and similar to your surroundings. Layered clothing provides comfort in changing weather conditions. A raincoat should be compact and lightweight so it will fit in your vest pocket and be available when it rains.

HATS

A fishing hat with a brim all the way around or with a long brim in front provides protection from the elements and some protection from errant casts. It can also help reduce surface glare and can be used for attaching magnifiers or lights to.

Flashlights

Lightweight pocketsize flashlights are essential if you fish at night. You may wish to consider clip-ons or similar lights for tying knots at night.

Landing Net

A landing net with a belly made of non-abrasive material will allow you to catch and release big fish more quickly than by hand, giving the fish a better chance of surviving.

Insect Net

Because it is difficult to determine the body color of a caddis, or to correctly match the size of a mayfly without close observation, many anglers also carry a small net (like ones used in aquariums) for catching insects. You can use these nets for matching the hatch. And when there is no hatch activity, you can use the net to collect samples of what the fish are eating below the surface.

Other Useful Accessories

• A **nipper** will trim the tag ends of your knots. Some come with built-in points for untangling knots and clearing glue from hook eyes.

•A **scissor-plier** combination is a handy tool for pinching split-shot, removing hooks, repairing gear, and making heavy cuts.

• A **thermometer** to check water temperature.

• A **hook sharpener** will sharpen hooks that are dulled by use. A sharp hook should grab the thumbnail without hesitation when pulled gently, as shown.

• A pair of **hemostats** will help you remove hooks.

• **Fly boxes** will help you keep your flies sorted and handy for onstream changes.

3 LINES

Line choices have dramatically increased in recent years. There are lines designed for particular species and situations, including a variety of floating and sinking line combinations with a wide range of sink rates.

While your local fly shop can give you good advice on lines—especially if it has guides who are willing to share their expertise—this chapter will cover most of your fishing situations.

HOW TO READ A FLY LINE BOX LABEL

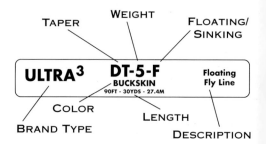

LINE RATINGS

Line ratings range from 1 to 15, with 1 being the lightest. Line numbers are assigned according to the weight of the first 30 feet of line, which is the length of an average cast. Thirty feet of a 6-weight line will properly load a 6-weight rod during the cast. Matching the weight of the line

and the rating of the rod creates a balanced outfit that will readily make a normal-length cast.

BASIC LINE TYPES

1. DOUBLE TAPER

Thin at both ends of the line, thicker toward
the middle. Versatile, roll casts effectively, mends
well. Can deliver a delicate presentation. Can
be reversed after one end wears, giving
two lines for the price of one. Thick middle
inhibits distance casting.

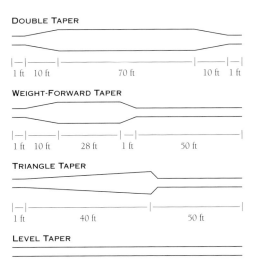

DOUBLE TAPER

|—|———|——————————————|———|—|
1 ft 10 ft   70 ft   10 ft 1 ft

WEIGHT-FORWARD TAPER

|—|———|—————|—|————————|
1 ft 10 ft   28 ft   1 ft   50 ft

TRIANGLE TAPER

|—|—————————————|————————|
1 ft   40 ft   50 ft

LEVEL TAPER

2. WEIGHT-FORWARD TAPER

(The most popular-selling line.) Thin at one
end, tapers to a thick section, then tapers back

down to a thin running line, which forms the longest section. Shoots well for longer casts. Takes less room on the reel than the same-weight double taper. Does not mend as well. Can only be fished with one end.

3. Triangle taper
(Developed by Lee Wulff.) Extremely long taper. Roll casts superbly. Can provide a very delicate presentation. Shoots well. Only one end can be used for fishing.

4. Level taper
No taper. Tends to kick downward at the end of the cast. Should not be considered worth the lower price.

5. Shooting head
Thirty to 38 feet of tapered line. Usually with a loop connection to attach separate running line. Used for long-distance casting and versatility.

6. Shooting line
Small-diameter, lightweight running line, used with shooting heads for distance casting.

7. Backing
Braided, supple, small-diameter line, used to extend line length and cushion line on the reel. Allows large fish to swim beyond the length of the fly line.

Choosing a Line

Most line manufacturers print brochures touting their current line's best uses. If you are not sure which taper you need, use the line manufacturers' literature to aid your selection. You might also ask your retailer to let you cast different lines, thereby choosing the one that you like best.

Your first line should be either a floating double-taper or weight-forward line. Whatever line you choose, keep in mind that different line types fit different situations, and don't be afraid to change lines.

Line Care

Fly lines are degraded by heat and preserved by cold. So avoid storing lines in a parked car on a sunny day. In the off-season, you can store them on the reel in a cool, dry place.

Although it is possible to wear out a line in a year—if you're fortunate to fish that much—a well-preserved and well-maintained line can last three to six years with normal use.

Insect repellent, gasoline, and most solvents will ruin a line in short order. In such cases the portion of the line that is handled is cracked and worn while the rest of the line is still in good condition. This is a sure sign that you're not being careful to remove insect repellent or other solvents from your hands before fishing. To protect your line, always apply insect repellent with the backs of your hands or use a stick-type repellent.

CLEANING

If your floating line begins to sink after some use, dirt and scum are probably the culprits. Clean line floats better and slides through the guides more smoothly for better shooting and playing of large fish.

For optimum performance, clean your line regularly. We recommend once every two or three outings—sooner if needed.

Most cleaning can be accomplished on the stream in a matter of seconds with a handy rag containing a small amount of mild hand soap. Simply run the used portion of the line through the rag. Commercial cleaning pads are also available for this purpose. Since some lines are coated with lubricating agents, and others are infused with lubricants designed to slowly leach to the surface during normal use, we suggest that you consult your manufacturer's recommendations for the best cleaning and maintenance techniques.

LINE TROUBLESHOOTING

FLOATING LINE SINKS

- Clean line per manufacturer instructions
- Replace line

LINE SURFACE CRACKS

- Clean hands carefully before handling line
- Avoid getting insect repellent on hands
- Store line in a cool place
- Replace line
- Try a different brand of line

KNOTS DO NOT HOLD

- Check knot procedure
- Replace line that may have degraded

DIFFICULT TO CAST

- Check if line weight matches rod
- Weighted flies are more difficult to cast
- Lightweight lines will be difficult in wind
- Get professional casting instruction

LINE MEMORY (GETTING OUT KINKS)

- Stretch line to straighten it
- Try other brands

4 LEADERS

The function of a leader is to dissipate the energy of the cast and allow a natural presentation of your fly to the fish. Its limpness and transparency disguise the fact that the fly is connected to your line.

Line diameter however is less likely to scare fish than stiffness. To prove that, Vince Marinaro inserted progressively larger diameters of monofilament pieces into floating beetles and dropped them onto the water without any observable effect on fish feeding behavior. Since the fish ate all the beetles regardless of the line diameter, he concluded that a natural drift was the key (see *In the Ring of the Rise* by V. Marinaro).

Generally, smaller flies require smaller-diameter leaders, while heavier flies cast better with stouter leaders.

DRY-FLY LEADERS

Most anglers agree that a dry fly is presented most effectively with a drag-free float—that is, when the fly floats "naturally," free of the drag caused by the current pulling against the tippet. To prevent drag as long as possible, the leader should have plenty of S curves when it lands. Since the fly floats on the surface, a taut leader is not required because you can immediately see the fish take, which allows you to set

DRY-FLY LEADER

the hook in time. You will know if your leader is right for a particular fly when you cast it and observe how it lands on the water.

WET-FLY LEADERS

Wet-fly leaders, on the other hand, should be designed so that nymphs or streamers drift near the bottom like the food being imitated. With a taut or nearly taut leader, the hook can be set

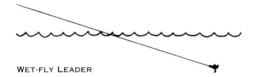

WET-FLY LEADER

when the take is felt. A quick set is important because trout will know almost immediately that a fly is not food and will spit it out. Also, underwater presentation of a streamer requires a short and taut leader to enable the angler to move the fly in a lifelike manner. Taking the time to adjust or change your leader for each situation will increase your success.

LENGTHS

For most situations, a 7½- to 9-foot tapered leader will catch fish. For extreme situations, leaders as short as 1 foot or as long as 15 feet are sometimes used. Shorter leaders are needed when fishing nymphs or streamers with a sink-tip line. They help get the fly down to the fish quickly in deep, fast water, and are good for casting in tight situations.

Extremely long leaders sacrifice accuracy but can improve dry-fly success in deep and/or clear water. In deeper water, fish have a wider field of vision at the surface and are more likely to see a nearby fly line (see chapter 8).

MONO OR BRAIDED

There are two types of commercial tapered leaders, mono and braided, which means that the butt section of the leader—the end that attaches to the fly line—is composed of either monofilament or a braided material. Braided leaders are more supple than their mono counterparts and therefore turn over very nicely. They're also very porous, which allows you to dress them to float or sink. On the other hand, they absorb water (which sprays the surface on a false cast) and dirt (which may makes them sink when you want them to float). Mono leaders are not porous, and are generally more popular than braided leaders. The following discussion refers to mono leaders, which we recommend.

TIPPET SIZE

Be cautious of charts or formulas that define required tippet size for a given hook size. While these can guide you in your initial selection, you must cast the fly and observe the results to determine if your choice was a good one. Wind resistance against the fly and tippet length are key factors.

The following chart shows the suggested range of fly sizes for each given tippet diameter. Notice the overlap. Notice also that if you add the tippet diameter to the corresponding X size you should always come up with the number 11. Remember this as the "Rule of 11."

TIPPET SIZE CHART

Tippet Diameter	X Size	# Test	Hook Size
.011"	0X	6.5	4–2/0
.010"	1X	5.5	2–8
.009"	2X	4.5	6–10
.008"	3X	3.8	8–14
.007"	4X	3.1	10–16
.006"	5X	2.4	12–16
.005"	6X	1.4	14–22
.004"	7X	1.1	18–28
.003"	8X	.75	18 & up

COMMERCIAL LEADERS

Though you can purchase quality commercially made tapered leaders through any fly-fishing shop or catalog, commercial leaders are limited to general-purpose use. You may find that building your own leaders will fit your fishing strategies better than commercial leaders. Modifying commercial leaders by adding butt sections or different tippets can also help.

CUSTOM LEADERS

Though sometimes an alteration in the casting stroke can compensate for a leader's deficiencies, it's easier to put the fly where you want it if you have the proper leader. The following chart will help you understand the requirements of leader building, which you can do yourself by tying together various lengths of different-diameter monofilament. Small length changes in leader formulas can usually be made by keeping the same proportions and changing the length of each piece.

George Harvey developed his first set of leader formulas based on the principle that many S curves are needed to prevent drag on the fly (see *Techniques of Trout Fishing and Fly Tying* by George W. Harvey). Note that the transition between hard and soft mono occurs between 2X (.009" diameter) and 3X (.008 diameter).

GEORGE HARVEY LEADER FORMULAS

		Dry Fly 10'6"(4X)	Dry Fly 11'(5X)	Wet Fly 9'(4X)	Brush 7'6"(4X)	
Hard Mono		10"	10"	12"	10"	.017"
		20"	20"	20"	14"	.015"
		20"	20"	—	14"	.013"
	0X	20"	20"	20"	10"	.011"
	2X	12"	12"	22"	10"	.009"
Soft Mono	3X	18"	12"	22"	12"	.008"
	4X	22–28"	18"	22"	16–20"	.007"
	5X	—	22–30"	—	—	.006"
	6X	—	—	—	—	.005"

X Size   Diameter

LEADER TROUBLESHOOTING

FISH REFUSES FLY

- Lengthen leader
- Use finer tippet

DRY-FLY LEADER SINKS

- Clean leader and apply flotant
- Check if leader construction matches fly

DRY-FLY LEADER STRAIGHTENS

- Lengthen tippet or use smaller size
- Check leader construction
- Use larger fly

LEADER COLLAPSES AT END OF CAST

- Shorten or stiffen tippet
- Check leader construction
- Use a smaller fly

WET-FLY LEADER WILL NOT SINK

- Add small split shot
- Add sinking stuff to coat leader

LEADER BREAKS ON A LARGE FISH

- Check leader for wear
- Check knot procedure
- Use larger tippet

5 KNOTS

There is nothing more aggravating than putting everything together for a successful hook-up, then losing a fish due to a poorly tied knot. We have therefore selected the best knots to cover all the basic connections from fly to reel. While a few are multipurpose, most are best suited for specific situations.

Note: You'll save valuable time on the water by practicing and learning knots in advance.

KEY TERMS

The section of the line from the knot to the end of the line is called the "tag end," which is usually trimmed after the knot is pulled tight. The "standing" part of the line is what remains of your line between knots.

BASIC PRINCIPLES

- To help your line slide and seat properly, always lubricate your knots before tightening. The easiest way is to use saliva.

- Knots seat best when tightened smoothly and steadily. Pulling too quickly can cause a knot to seat improperly, and can create unnecessary friction that weakens the knot.

- Be careful to trim excess material as close as possible without damaging the knot or line. This not only provides a neater appearance but allows the knot to perform better for casting, and to pass more smoothly through the rod guides.

- Be sure to inspect your leaders for abrasion, wind knots, or other damage that may cause the fish of a lifetime to break free.

- Be sure to remove any tippet material that may be curled or damaged from a previous fly before tying on another.

- Most knots slip before they fail. Be sure the knot is fully seated and you will reduce your knot failures.

- If your line breaks on a fish or snag, examine it. If there are small curls at the end of the line, the knot failed.

Aside from damaged line or weak knots at other points, the tippet is typically the weakest section of any leader. The ability to tie consistent, quality knots where the fly is attached to the tippet and the tippet is attached to the leader is crucial.

Note: Practice is the only way to tie consistent, quality knots that will continue to perform well.

FLY TO TIPPET

CLINCH KNOT

One of the most common knots, the clinch is very simple to tie but difficult to seat with heavier lines and therefore shouldn't be used with lines testing greater than 12 pounds. To

maintain consistent strength, 5 turns are recommended for lines up to 6-pound test, 4 turns
for 6- to 12-pound test.

Thread 6 to 8 inches of line through the eye of
the hook.

Bring the tag end back toward the standing line,
creating a loop at the eye of the hook. Pinch

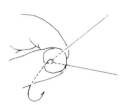

your left thumb and
forefinger around the
hook eye to preserve
the loop. The knot
is easier to finish if
you allow for a
larger opening.

Make 4 or 5 turns (depending on the pound
test) with the tag end around the standing part
of the line. When making your turns, rotate

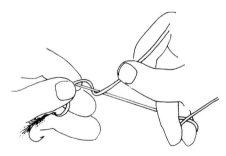

your hands over and under the standing part
of the line, passing the tag end from the
thumb and forefinger of your right hand to

the middle and fourth fingers of your left. This method allows you to keep tension on the standing part of the line.

Push the tag end of the line through the small loop created at the hook eye. Make sure the tag end stays in the loop by holding it with the thumb and forefinger of your left hand.

Lubricate the knot and pull on the hook and standing part of the line to seat the knot. Trim the tag end.

GEORGE HARVEY KNOT

Developed by legendary fly-fishing instructor George Harvey, this knot allows small flies and flies with turned-up or turned-down eyes to ride naturally on the water and is not recommended for hooks with ring eyes.

Insert about 6 inches of tippet through the front of the hook eye. Hold the tag end and standing part together in front of the fly. (It is not necessary to hold the fly until tightening the knot.)

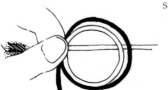

With the tag end, make two circles about the size of a dime around the standing part of the line. While holding the circles together with the thumb and forefinger of the left hand, pass the tag end through the circles twice.

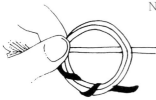

Now start to tighten the knot by holding the hook and pulling on the standing part of the tippet.

Lubricate the knot and tighten until the circles jump over the hook eye. The knot is tied wrong if the circles do not pass over the hook eye.

Seat the knot completely and trim the tag end.

NON-SLIP LOOP

Using a loop will allow your fly to swing freely, and is especially useful in providing a more natural drift when fishing nymphs or small dry flies. As its name suggests, the non-slip loop is very strong and won't slip toward the hook eye.

Again, it is important to use the correct number of turns for the line weight being used. Seven turns for lines to 6 pounds, 5 turns for 8- to 12-pound line, 4 turns for 15- to 40-pound line, and 3 turns for 50- to 60-pound line.

Begin this knot by tying an overhand knot in the line about 12 inches from the end. (You can reduce this as you become proficient in tying the knot.) Pass the tag end through the hook eye and back through the loop created by the over- hand knot. Be  sure that the tag end goes through the same side of the overhand knot that it came out on.

Like the clinch knot, make the appropriate number of turns around the standing part and pass the tag end back through the overhand knot on the same side that it last exited.

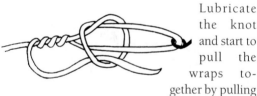 Lubricate the knot and start to pull the wraps to- gether by pulling on the tag end. Before the wraps are completely tight, pull on the hook and standing part to fin- ish seating the knot.

TIPPET TO LEADER AND LEADER SECTIONS

SURGEON'S KNOT

Simply a double overhand knot tied with two pieces of line, the surgeon's knot is very easy to tie and is popular for joining tippets to leaders, and for tying finer leader sections.

It is quicker, stronger, and easier to tie than the blood knot but will not allow the line to lie as straight and is therefore not as popular for tying leader sections. It does however work better than the blood knot in tying lines that vary greatly in diameter.

With the leader in your left hand and the tippet in your right, overlap about 4 to 6 inches of the end of the leader with the end of the tippet. Using your right hand,  make an overhand knot with both lines. This will create a loop.

Make a double overhand knot by  passing the line and tippet through the loop created in step one.

You will now have the tag end of the tippet and the standing part of the leader in your left hand, and the tag end of the leader and standing part of the tippet in your right. Lu-bricate the knot and tighten by pulling on all four strands at the same time. Pulling the individual strands before trimming the knot will ensure that it's tightly seated.

BLOOD KNOT (BARREL KNOT)

With a little practice, the blood knot is easier to tie than it looks. Many anglers prefer to use it for leader sections because of its smooth, low profile, which allows the knot to travel easily through rod guides. The blood knot, however, doesn't work well for lines that vary greatly in diameter.

Cross both pieces of line at 90 degree angles, forming an X and leaving 6 inches of tag end for each line. Hold the intersection between the thumb and forefinger of your left hand and make 5 turns with the tag end on the right side around the standing part of the line.

It is helpful to use the same technique for wrapping as described in the clinch knot: hold the tag end between the third and fourth fingers of the left hand and rotate your hands over and under the standing part of the line as you pass the tag end to your thumb and forefinger of the right hand. Pass the tag end to the other side of the intersection of lines.

Change directions by pinching the intersection of the lines and the tag end that has passed the intersection with your right thumb and forefinger. Make 5 turns with the remaining tag end around the standing part of the left side. Now

5

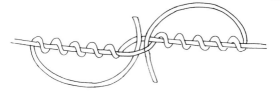

pass this tag end through the intersection of the lines, but in the opposite direction of the first tag end.

Lubricate and pull on the standing parts to seat the knot, being careful not to let the tag ends slip out. Until you gain some proficiency, it may be helpful to hold the tag ends in your teeth, without pulling on them, as you tighten the knot.

DROPPER TO LEADER

Fishermen have been using multiple lures or baits on a single line for centuries. Fly fishermen are no exception. By adding a dropper fly to your line you can increase your chances of catching fish.

CLINCH KNOT

The easiest way to accomplish this is by connecting a second fly to the fly at the end of your tippet.

Using a clinch knot, simply tie a second piece of tippet to the eye or bend of your first fly's hook. Tie your dry fly on first if you intend to use both dry and wet flies. The dry fly will act as a strike indicator if there is a strike on the wet fly.

DROPPER LOOP KNOT

The dropper loop is an excellent choice for attaching a second fly. It can be used as a loop for attaching a second section of line with a loop-to-loop connection, or one end of the loop can be cut by the standing part of the line, leaving a single strand for attaching a fly.

Decide where you want to add the dropper and make a circle in your line. The bigger the circle, the bigger the loop.

While pinching the intersection of the loop, wrap the loop around itself 3 or 4 times.

5

Pull the outside edge of the loop through the center of the wraps twice.

Lubricate the knot and pull on the standing part of the line to seat the loop. There is no need to pull on the loop as it will form itself.

LEADER TO FLY LINE

There are many times when a change in tactics will require you to change your leader. Many anglers who use a knot for this connection will generally replace only their tippet section, or first two leader sections, before replacing a leader. Because the entire leader contributes to the performance of your cast, changing only these sections can decrease your ability to properly present your fly.

To facilitate leader changes, many anglers prefer to use a loop-to-loop connection, and some popular lines and leaders come with loop connectors built in. We offer the loop-to-loop connection here, along with a couple of knots that will allow you to tie loop connections for lines and leaders that come without loops from the manufacturer.

But first we offer the tweed clinch knot, which we believe to be one of the best and easiest knot for attaching the leader to the fly line and the fly line to the backing.

TWEED CLINCH KNOT

Hold the fly line and leader so that they overlap about eight inches, with the leader or backing in your left hand.

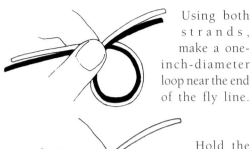

Using both strands, make a one-inch-diameter loop near the end of the fly line.

Hold the loop between your left thumb and forefinger. Bring the tag end of the leader toward you through the loop five times.

Straighten the fly line and keep it taut. Slide the knot into final position, then tighten by pulling both ends of the leader until the knot is snug, being sure to keep the wraps together. Fully set this knot before trimming by holding the line and leader over your thighs and

gently spreading your knees to create more tension than you can generate with just your hands.

Note: This knot does not require lubrication.

BRAIDED LOOP CONNECTOR

Braided loops can be purchased from many sources and attached to the end of your fly line for a strong connection. They allow you to easily replace an entire leader without having to retie a knot at the fly line. Using heat and/or glue, they can be easily replaced if worn.

LOOP-TO-LOOP CONNECTION

While this connection is most popular for attaching the leader to the fly line, it is also used to attach monofilament tippets to a base leader section attached to the fly line. This allows you to quickly change tippets as well as the entire leader when needed.

Because the loop-to-loop connection is easy to flub, the following illustration shows both the right and wrong way to connect the loops.

CORRECT LOOP-TO-LOOP CONNECTION

INCORRECT LOOP-TO-LOOP CONNECTION

To do it the right way, insert the fly line loop through the loop in the butt of the leader. Then pass the tippet end of the leader completely through

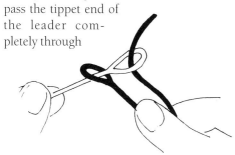

the fly line loop. Pull on the fly line and leader to tighten the connection. The knot will continue to seat itself through continued use. Pushing the leader and fly line toward each other will allow you to disconnect the loops.

PERFECTION LOOP

One of the most popular knots for making an end loop, this knot can be tied with very little practice. Unlike the surgeon's loop, this loop seats directly in line with the standing part of the leader.

Hold the leader butt between the thumb and forefinger of your left hand about 6 inches from the tag end. Make a loop in the line with the tag end passing behind the standing part and ending up on the right side. Hold the loop between the thumb and forefinger of your left hand.

Make a second loop, smaller than the first, by passing the tag end in front of the first loop, around the back of the first loop, ending up with the tag end on the right side. Hold both loops with the thumb and forefinger of your left hand.

Lay the tag end, from right to left, between the two loops and hold it between your thumb and forefinger.

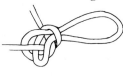

From behind the first loop, grab the second loop and pull it through the first. Lubricate the knot and continue to seat the loop by holding the standing part of the leader with your left hand and pulling on the loop with your right. Inserting the end of a pair of hemostats or pliers through the loop will give you leverage to help tighten the knot.

SURGEON'S LOOP

The surgeon's loop is basically the surgeon's knot tied with only one line. While not quite as neat as the perfection loop, the surgeon's loop is easier to tie.

Form a loop by doubling the tag end back over the standing part of the leader with about 6 inches of overlap. Make an overhand knot in the double line. Bring the loop through the overhand knot again to create a double overhand knot.

Lubricate and seat the knot by holding the tag end and standing part of the leader with one

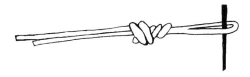

hand and pulling on the loop with the other. The end of hemostats or pliers inserted through the loop will help seat the knot firmly.

FLY LINE TO BACKING
(see Tweed Clinch)

BACKING TO REEL
Because you are more likely to break at the tippet before getting down this far, this connection is one that is rarely tested. We have nonetheless selected the arbor knot because of its reliability. If this knot breaks, you have probably

tied it wrong. Make sure it's properly seated. If it does fail you'll have an excellent fish story to replace the line you've lost.

ARBOR KNOT

Circle the arbor of the reel with the tag end of your backing twice and tie an overhand knot around the standing part of the line. Make sure the tag end and standing part of the line come out of the same reel pillars.

Tie a second overhand knot in the tag end of the fly line. Moisten both the line and knots and tighten by holding the reel in one hand and the standing part of the fly line in the other. As you seat the knot, the second overhand knot will draw down to the first and create a jam to prevent the knot from slipping.

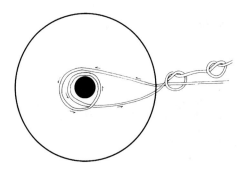

Be sure to reel the backing on tightly. This and the two initial wraps around the reel will prevent the backing from slipping on the spool.

TYING IT UP

FLY LINE TO BACKING
• Tweed Clinch Knot

BACKING TO REEL
• Arbor Knot

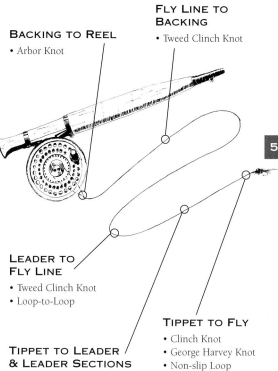

5

LEADER TO FLY LINE
• Tweed Clinch Knot
• Loop-to-Loop

TIPPET TO FLY
• Clinch Knot
• George Harvey Knot
• Non-slip Loop

TIPPET TO LEADER & LEADER SECTIONS
• Surgeon's Knot
• Blood Knot

6 CASTING

Casting can be as simple as understanding these three basic principles:

1. THE END OF THE LINE MUST BE MOVING TO BEGIN ANY CAST.

If there is slack in the line you'll waste energy and be unable to "load" the rod properly, by which we mean bringing the weight of the line to bear against the rod, causing it to bend like a spring.

Thus always begin a backcast with the rod tip low, and strip out any slack in the line. When making a forward cast, begin your stroke just before the backcast is completely unrolled, while the end of the line is still moving. If the backcast unrolls completely, the end of the line will stop and the rod will not load properly.

2. YOU MUST RAPIDLY ACCELERATE THEN STOP THE ROD IN A *SHORT* DISTANCE.

This part of the cast determines loop size. Accelerating to a stop in a short distance generates a tight loop. A longer acceleration move yields a wider loop. Think of this part of the cast as forcing a bend in the rod by pushing against the inertia of the line, then stopping so the unbending rod propels the line to the target.

3. THE LINE WILL TRAVEL IN THE DIRECTION THE ROD TIP WAS MOVING BEFORE YOU STOPPED THE ROD.

This principle allows you to watch your line during a cast and adjust your stroke so that your line goes where you want it. When casting for fish, all your concentration should be on the target. When practicing or developing a new cast, however, it is helpful to watch the line to improve your timing and hone your stroke.

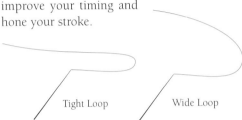

6

Tight Loop   Wide Loop

GRIP

Proper casting grip requires the thumb on top of the handle, with fingers encircling the rod grip. The thumb is used as a fulcrum and pointer.

The grip should only be tight during the acceleration-and-stop part of the cast, the rest of the time it should be relaxed, just tight enough to hold the rod. Blisters from casting indicate that your grip is too tight.

LINE CONTROL

Use your other hand to grab the line and hold it waist-level in front of you. Your line hand will enable you to gain additional control of the line as you cast.

STANCE

Stand with your casting-side foot slightly back (right foot back if you are right-handed).

Keep your wrist stiff. Your forearm is a stronger lever than your wrist, so by keeping your wrist stiff you're using your best leverage, and therefore less effort. Proper casting requires minimal physical exertion. Let your elbow move, don't try to keep it pressed to your side.

BACKCAST

The basic cast begins with the backcast, which requires that 15 to 20 feet of line be extended from the rod tip.

Start with the rod tip low, near the surface of the water. Remove all slack and get the end of the line moving before beginning the backcast.

Slowly pull the rod toward you until the line is off the water, then accelerate quickly to a stop. If the line makes a ripping sound as it leaves

6

the water you're moving too quickly in the first part of the stroke.

Your line will travel in the direction the rod tip is traveling when you accelerate and stop the rod. The direction of your backcast loop will tell you if you need to adjust your stopping point.

FORWARD CAST

The forward cast
begins where your
backcast ends,
when the line has a
J shape and is not
fully unrolled be-
hind you. At this

point,
the same
s t r o k e
used on the
backcast is
made in the direc-
tion of the target. Your thumb-print should be
facing the target while your thumb is exerting

the maximum pressure needed for rapid acceleration to a stop. After the line straightens, gently lower your rod tip and let the line fall to the water.

Again, to load the rod properly the end of the line must be moving.

6

ROLL CAST
Roll casts are used when wind or obstructions prevent a normal backcast. Begin the roll cast like a regular cast, with your line straightened out on the water. Now tilt your rod back until your line is behind your shoulder.

Then make a normal forward cast from this position. For a longer roll cast, move the

casting arm farther back before making the cast. A slight pause before the forward cast aids in loading the rod.

FALSE CAST

False casting is the regular cast done without allowing the fly to land. It is used to dry a fly, measure distance, work out additional line needed for a longer cast, or to learn the timing of an outfit.

REACH CAST

The reach cast is commonly used to extend the drag-free drift of a dry fly when casting across the current. It is also used to keep the line from landing over the fish when casting directly upstream.

Make your forward cast. Before the line falls to the water, point the rod tip upstream (or, when casting upstream, to the right or left of the fish) and lower it, releasing line from your line hand at the same time.

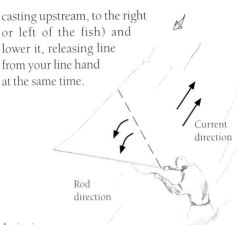

Current direction

Rod direction

It is important that about ten feet of line be held loose in your line hand, because if line is not released, the distance of the cast will be shortened.

MENDING

When faster currents at midstream create a curve or "belly" in the line, the drag-free float can be extended by mending line. Simply flip the rod tip upstream

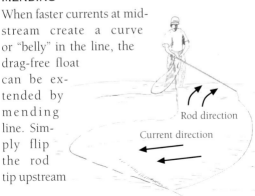

Rod direction

Current direction

51

in a semicircular motion with less force than a regular cast. The idea is to move the belly portion of the line without disturbing the fly.

HAULING

Hauling is a technique used to add line speed, and therefore distance, to your cast. It is also useful when casting in heavy wind. It consists of a short pull with the line hand during the acceleration stroke. A double haul consists of using a haul on the backcast and forward cast.

SIDEARM CAST

This is the basic cast done with your arm extended parallel to the ground, allowing you to get under obstructions or avoid wind.

SHOOTING AND STRIPPING LINE

Often done in conjunction with hauling, shooting line entails releasing line after the rod tip has stopped on the cast, thereby lengthening the cast. It helps to drop the rod tip before releasing the line.

The line must be stripped from the reel and held in your line hand prior to shooting.

Whether shooting or stripping, it is important to maintain control of the line so that you are always ready for a strike. Shoot line through a loop made by your line-hand thumb and fore-finger. When stripping, transfer the line under a finger of your casting hand and strip from be-hind your casting hand.

CASTING WITH WIND
FROM YOUR CASTING SIDE
Make a sidearm backcast wide and as low as space allows. Then make a normal forward cast.

CASTING WITH WIND
FROM YOUR OPPOSITE SIDE
Make a low backcast on your upwind side, then make a normal forward cast. The acceleration-and-stop part of the cast is the same.

CASTING INTO THE WIND

Make a higher-than-normal backcast and a lower-than-normal forward cast.

Aim your cast so that your leader unrolls just above the water's surface. Your fly is most vulnerable to wind after the leader unrolls and the energy of the cast dissipates, so the trick is to shorten the distance the fly drops to the water. A higher forward cast will allow your fly to be blown off target.

Again, hauling is also useful for casting into the wind (see *Hauling* earlier in this chapter).

CASTING WITH WIND FROM BEHIND

Make a low backcast, reaching the rod well back to begin the forward cast. This longer reach allows you, when making the forward cast, to remove any slack in the line caused by the wind. Aim the forward cast high for increased distance.

CASTING TIPS

- When making any cast, the rod tip must quickly accelerate and stop. This allows the rod action (unbending of the rod) to propel the line in the direction the rod tip was moving when you stopped your casting motion. Moving the rod tip at a constant velocity will not load the rod. Move the rod fast enough so that the inertia of the line creates a bend in the rod, then stop quickly, allowing the straightening rod to propel the line.

- The speed and power of the backcast should match the speed and power of the forward cast. A weak backcast will not allow you to make an effective forward cast.

- Move the rod farther if you need more distance or line speed.

- To develop the timing of your acceleration stroke, practice with your line hand in your pocket and hold the line fixed with the fingers of your casting hand. Practice your stroke with the length of line that is easiest for you to cast, don't try for distance.

CASTING TROUBLESHOOTING

TAILING LOOPS (LINE CROSSES ITSELF)

- Drop the rod tip slightly after stopping the rod
- Apply power evenly on the acceleration stroke

WIDE LOOPS

- Shorten your acceleration move
- Drop the rod tip less after the stop
- Keep wrist stiff

LINE POPS ON BACKCAST

- Allow backcast to unroll farther

DIFFICULTY WITH LONGER CASTS

- Move arm farther back on the backcast
- Make a stronger backcast
- Begin forward cast just before backcast unrolls completely, when line is J-shaped
- Practice acceleration stroke on shorter line and gradually increase casting length; the timing changes with more line out
- Keep the elbow below shoulder height on the backcast

LINE HITS WATER ON BACKCAST

- Remove all slack before starting the backcast
- Keep your wrist stiff
- Stop the rod tip sooner on the backcast
- Begin forward cast just before backcast is completely unrolled

PRACTICE

Support your investment in rod, reel, and gear with casting practice. Follow the principles discussed in this chapter and you will improve your accuracy and distance.

Critique your own casting by observing your casting loop. Your loop will travel in the direction that you accelerate and stop the rod tip. A wide loop is caused by longer acceleration stroke.

For more advice on casting, read *The Cast* by Ed Jaworowski.

And remember, it is much easier to correct a casting fault, or develop a new cast, on your lawn than with a large fish in sight.

6

7 SELECTING FLIES

To catch fish you'll need to:

1) Select a fly that imitates the size, shape, and color of the food fish are eating.

2) Make your artificial fly behave like the real thing.

Both require a basic understanding of entomology—the study of bugs. Knowing, for instance, that aquatic insects have an underwater stage can be very helpful when fish aren't taking the bugs floating on the water's surface. Moreover, insect life varies not only from region to region and stream to stream but within a given stream as well: some forms of insects thrive in fast currents and others thrive in slower currents and pools. Knowing what to look for can increase your interest and your success.

This chapter will give you an overview of the insects most commonly available to trout, and will help you make sense of your own onstream observations. Whenever possible, catch an insect that's flying over the stream, floating on the water, hanging on streamside vegetation, or hiding under rocks on the stream's bottom and examine it closely to determine which fly to use.

Be sure to look for the following characteristics:

SHAPE

Insect shapes vary greatly between orders and between nymphal and adult stages. The more selective the trout, the more important it is to match the shape of the fly with the natural insect. Your best bet is to match the shape first, then alter the size or color of the fly to get as close as possible to the natural.

SIZE

When there are multiple insects available at one time, an exact size match may not be required. However, if one insect predominates, matching size can be critical. Again, the more selective the trout, the more important size becomes. By the same token, an exact size match is more important when using smaller flies, because a wrong-size small fly is more noticeable to trout.

Fly sizes correspond with hook sizes, with trout flies generally ranging from #18 to #10.

COLOR

Though color can be the most difficult characteristic to match, you'll have to come fairly close to fool very selective trout. When possible, catch an insect that is currently active on the stream and examine it closely. Color can be hard to determine at long distances, especially when the underside of an emerger or dun is a different color than the portion of the insect above the water.

7

BEHAVIOR

Because the nymphs and adults of each order behave differently underneath, at the surface, or out of the water, you'll need to employ different strategies when imitating them. For instance, some nymphs are active swimmers, while others simply float with little or no movement. Know the differences and present your flies accordingly.

AQUATIC INSECTS

Aquatic insects, which make up the bulk of a trout's diet, begin life as eggs on the stream bottom then grow through larval and/or pupal stages, emerging from the water as adults to mate, deposit eggs back to the water, and perish. However short and unglamorous their lives might seem, these insects are extremely important to trout and thus to the fly fisher. Mayflies,

The life cycle of a mayfly.

caddisflies, stoneflies, and midges form the key insect groups.

MAYFLIES

Mayflies have a three-stage life cycle, changing from nymphs to duns to adults.

NYMPHS

There are four types of mayfly nymphs: swimmers, clingers, burrowers, and crawlers.

Mayfly Nymph

Swimmers

Slim, streamlined and long-tailed, swimmers often emerge in open water on overcast and rainy days. Look

Hare's Ear

for them around logs and rocks, where many of them will crawl before hatching into the air, and around vegetation. Impart some action to your nymph retrieve to mimic their swimming.

Clingers

Flat-bodied, with eyes on top of their heads, clingers usually live in the faster water of runs and riffles but will migrate to slower waters or eddies behind rocks and logs before hatching. Susceptible to pollution, they will normally be found where water quality is high. They don't swim well, so present your imitation with a dead drift. Many will emerge from their shucks prior to drifting any distance and require you to imitate the emerging mayfly rather than the nymph.

Burrowers

Three-tailed, and somewhat flat-bodied like their clinger cousins, burrowers have tusk-like mandibles that aid their burrowing. You can find them in quieter areas like back eddies, where silt, mud, and sand predominate, and on the slower streams of the East and Midwest—but usually not until after dark, when they come out to feed or emerge. A twitching retrieve that imitates their swimming can be productive during such times.

Crawlers

Stocky, three-tailed, with eyes on the sides of their wide heads, crawlers generally are poor swimmers and move about the stream bottom on their legs.

You can find them in moderate to fast currents, usually among debris, vegetation, rocks, boulders, and logs on the stream bottom, but they prefer gravel, gathering food between stones while staying sheltered from enemies. Like clingers, many crawlers will migrate to slower water before emergence. A dead-drift presentation is most effective.

EMERGERS

This transitional stage between nymph and dun—in which the nymph is struggling to emerge from its nymphal shuck—marks the beginning of what fly fishers refer to as the "hatch." Splashy rises could be the result of trout trying to take emergers before they escape from the surface film. Bulge rises could mean that trout are taking emergers below the surface. Start with an emerger pattern but be prepared to switch to a dun as soon as trout start feeding on the surface.

DUNS

The newly emerged "dun," as it's called, will float on the current until its wings dry, during which time it resembles a tiny sailboat (wings

Hair Wing

upright like miniature sails) and is most vulnerable to trout. Be sure to present your fly ahead of the line and leader, because trout usually have time for a good look. Also, be sure to fish your fly with a drag-free drift. If that doesn't seem to work, try twitching the fly to make it look like it's struggling to escape its nymphal shuck.

ADULTS/SPINNERS

In this final stage, mayflies molt then take to the air with translucent wings to mate, after which the female deposits her eggs on the water and dies.

Mayfly Adult

The spent insects lie still with their wings flat on the water's surface, where trout often take them with

Adams

slow, methodical rises. Large clouds of mayflies in the air near dusk are a good indication of a coming spinner fall. Look for spinners in pools and flat areas, and be sure to fish quality imitations using a drag-free drift because trout will have time for a good look.

Mayfly Spinner

Spinner

CADDISFLIES

Caddisflies have what is considered a complete metamorphosis, progressing from egg to larvae to pupae to adult.

LARVAE

Caddis larvae resemble miniature worms and are divided into two distinct groups, case-building and free-living.

Case-building Larvae

Most caddis larvae build homes—out of sand, gravel, small twigs, and vegetation—which they carry around with them for protection from small predators and to help camouflage them from bottom-feeding fish. These larvae are wormlike in appearance and have six short legs that protrude from their cases; they can be found on the undersides of submerged rocks. Trout will eat them case and all. Try using a dead-drift presentation in medium and slow water.

Case-building Larva

Caseworm

7

Free-living Larvae

Free-living larvae hide in gravel, rocks, and debris on the stream bottom. While some roam freely, others build small nets over entrances to their gravel retreats and use them to trap food from the current. Also worm-like in appearance, their soft bodies afford little protection and they rely on hiding and secrecy for survival. They are a more readily available food source than case-builders, and you can find them in the faster waters of riffles and runs. Try a dead-drift presentation near the bottom.

Caddis Larva

PUPAE

It is during the pupal stage that the caddis undergoes the transformation from larvae to adult. Case-builders attach their cases to the bottom and change inside while free-living larvae either build a cocoon or change within their retreats. This stage is not very important to the angler.

EMERGERS

Caddis often emerge in open water at dusk or shortly after dark, rising with the assistance of trapped gases and breaking from their pupal skins. Emerging caddis rise faster than almost all other insects, sometimes bouncing, jumping, and skittering across the surface as they try to get airborne. Trout often take caddis emergers exclusively during a hatch and tend to concentrate on rising emergers below or at the surface.

Sparkle Pupa

Slashing, aggressive rises, sometimes airborne, are often an indicator that trout are taking caddis emergers. Soft hackle flies, which imitate the parts of wing cases, legs, and antennae, work best. Present them with a rising action.

ADULTS

Adult caddis have distinctive, tent-shaped wings and are mothlike in appearance. Unlike mayflies, some caddis will mate several times, after which the females deposit their eggs back

Caddis Adult

to the water. Look for adult caddis that seem to dive into or bounce on the water's surface; the Grannom fly, with its green egg-sack, can be very productive. Caddis imitations also make excellent searching patterns when little insect activity is evident. Try a drag-free presentation, and if that

Elk Hair Caddis

doesn't work, try twitching your fly. Trout that do take adults will make splashy, violent strikes.

Henryville Caddis

For more information, read Gary LaFontaine's *Caddisflies*. It is the most complete account of everything you need to know about caddisflies.

STONEFLIES

Though most abundant in the faster, rockier streams out West, stoneflies can be found throughout the country. Stoneflies have a two-stage life cycle, progressing from nymph to adult with no intermediate pupal stage.

STONEFLY NYMPHS

Stonefly nymphs have two tails, distinct wing cases, and two claws at the end of each leg. Nymphs range widely in size and can live from one to three years, making them a consistently available food source. Imitations work best when presented near the stream bottom. Because stonefly nymphs emerge above the waterline, the best fishing

Stonefly Nymph

occurs a week or two prior to emergence, when nymphs are migrating toward shore.

Montana Nymph

ADULTS

Adult stoneflies retain their two nymphal tails and have wings that lie flat along their backs. They mate in streamside vegetation, after which the female drops her eggs from the air or dislodges them by dropping to the water. Present your fly along shore during the day and in the main current at dusk or after dark, which is when egg-laying usu-

Stonefly Adult

ally occurs. Use dead-drift presentations first, then impart some twitches if you have no strikes.

A slap cast can sometimes attract trout by imitating a crashing female stonefly trying to deposit her eggs. It is often better to try other insect imitations—unless you witness feeding activity or nymph migration—before going to the stonefly.

MIDGES

Though the term "midge" has come to be the fly fisher's catch-all for just about any small fly, more specifically it refers to Chironomids, the gnatlike flies found in nearly all trout waters, though most abundantly in slower moving streams and lakes with heavy plant growth and silty, soft bottoms. Midge hatches often break the rule that the size of the food organism is

7

proportional to the size of the fish that will pursue it. Large concentrations of hatching midges make it worthwhile for larger trout to pursue them. Midges are available year-round, so try fishing them when mayflies, caddisflies, and stoneflies are as not active. Like caddis, midges go through a complete metamorphosis.

LARVAE

Small and wormlike, midge larvae come in a variety of colors. They float freely in the current, so use a drag-free presentation.

PUPAE

Pupae are most im-
portant to the angler
during their emer-
gence, when large

Midge Pupa

numbers hang at the water's surface. Gas bubbles trapped in their pupal skins—important visual cues to trout and therefore imitated in fly patterns—help raise them slowly to the surface where their pupal skin splits and they fly away.

Pupa Fly

Calm days with smooth water make it harder for the insects to break through the surface tension. This can mean quite a smorgasbord for trout. At such times it is often difficult to entice a trout to take a single fly; try presenting your fly among insects massing over visible rises. Use a dead-drift presentation in shallow water and a slow retrieve in deeper water. Suspect emerging midges when you see rising trout but can't see what they are feeding on.

Griffith's Gnat

ADULTS

Adult midges have two wings, no tails, and plumelike antennae. After emergence they fly to nearby vegetation where they will wait a day or two before they are ready to mate, during which they can be seen flying in swarms above the water, sometimes at pretty fair heights. Egg-laying can occur just about anywhere. Some eggs are deposited on structures where larvae will fall to the water after hatching, others will be deposited at the water's surface, and still others will be taken to the bottom by struggling females.

Midge Adult

7

TERRESTRIALS

Terrestrial insects are an important food source for trout, especially in the second half of summer when the most common aquatic hatches are slowing down. Many times a trout only mildly interested in feeding will take a terrestrial that floats by.

Terrestrials do not willingly go into the water but often fall or get blown from streamside trees, brush, and other vegetation. For this reason they are more commonly found along the water's edge, particularly in areas of overhanging vegetation. Terrestrials are often more available to trout when air temperatures rise into the upper seventies and beyond, and when winds and rain are strong enough to blow them into the water. Grasshoppers, ants, and beetles are both readily available and easily recognized, making them favorites of trout and fly fishers.

GRASSHOPPERS

Grasshopper imitations work best during midday when aquatic insects are less active, and during late summer when the hatches  are waning and hoppers have grown to nice-sized meals. Because grasshoppers use their legs to help propel them into flight, you won't find many flying off the water. Instead, they'll kick  and struggle for land, which is why twitching your hopper imitation can be very effective. Grasshoppers grow in a variety of

Dave's Hopper

sizes and colors. Finding out the type of hoppers that predominate where you fish will help determine your fly selection.

ANTS

Trout sometimes go out of their way to eat ants, even when food sources of other types are readily available. In the later half of the summer, migrating ants will take wing and provide fishing that can equal mayfly and caddis hatches. Though winged imitations are preferable, wingless imitations can be just as effective.

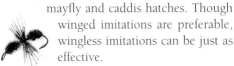

Ants come in a variety of sizes that can be matched by hooks from #28 to #10. Colors include black, brown, and dark reds.

BEETLES

On warm summer days when nothing seems to be happening, a beetle imita- tion may get a few fish to rise. Beetles are often clumsy fliers and will land on the water with a splash. Do the same with your fly to represent the natural. Fish beetles dead drift as they don't have a lot they can do while floating in the water.

7

ATTRACTORS

Attractor patterns usually aren't imitations of any specific food source but rather a combination of food characteristics meant to excite fish to

Humpy

strike. As such, most contain bright coloration, glitz, or exaggerated size to make them stand out and grab a fish's attention. Their ability to catch fish can't be disputed.

Use attractors when there is little insect activity. Fish already feeding on available foods can be hard to fool with attractors. Start with proven patterns— if attractor flies are too subtle, they may be perceived as a bad imitation of a natural; if they are too garrish, they may

Bivisible

simply be amusing to your quarry. Attractor flies often work well as searching patterns. Patterns that sit high on the water, like the Humpy or Bivisible, present themselves less clearly and may fool trout. Use a good amount of flotant to keep them sitting high. Using larger or bulkier flies in fast or rough water provides a clearer target for waiting fish. The fish will often commit to the take in order to capture your fly before it floats by. Presenting attractors with movement can sometimes help them get noticed.

OTHER FOODS

Minnows, crayfish, leeches, and even worms are just some of the other trout foods

Woolly Bugger

you can imitate with
streamers and other long,
sinking flies made of feathers and/or fur.

Matuka

TIPS FOR FISHING NYMPHS

- A trout's diet consists mostly of underwater meals: what may appear to be a
  surface rise could be a trout eating a
  nymph near the surface.

- Nymphs are always a good selection when
  there is no surface activity.

- Match your nymph type with the pre-
  dominant insects on the stream.

- Try to match the color of the nymph to
  the color of the stream bottom. Mother
  Nature tends to provide insects a defense
  by allowing them to camouflage themselves with their surroundings.

- Slow-moving nymphs provoke slow and
  deliberate feeding. Trout will conserve
  energy by letting the nymphs drift toward
  them.

- Swimming nymphs, or those that are on
  their way to emergence, will generally
  provoke more active strikes from trout
  trying to catch a meal before it flies
  away or gets back to some stream structure to hide.

7

- While some nymphs are active swimmers, almost all nymphs will drift inactively at some point. First, try a dead drift. If there are no takers, impart some action.

- Unless fishing emerger patterns, keep the fly as deep in the water as possible.

- If you are seeing feeding activity below the surface and nymph fishing has you stumped, switch to an emerger pattern.

- Be sure to periodically check your fly for vegetation or other debris that may cause a fish to reject your offering.

- Use nymph imitations in riffles where the largest populations of nymphs often occur, or in areas where two currents merge: fish will hold in slower water waiting for food to drift by in the faster current.

- Use a strike indicator, which floats on the water's surface like a bobber and will bob, pause, or sink when a fish strikes, helping you detect underwater strikes before the fish spits your fly.

GENERAL TIPS

- When not matching the hatch, try a pattern proven to catch fish in your location.

- Try using attractor patterns and terrestrials when no hatch activity is present.

- Try an attractor pattern if natural imitations don't seem to work.

- If takes are few and far between, changing flies after 6 to 10 casts will help you find a pattern that works.

- If feeding trout continue to refuse your offering, change to a fly that represents a different stage. Fish that appear to be rising but refusing your dun imitation may be feeding exclusively on the emerger.

- Stream conditions, weather, time of day, and time of year all contribute to changes in trout feeding behavior.

- Patterns like the Elk Hair Caddis, Adams, and Woolly Bugger make excellent searcher patterns.

7

- It pays to have several patterns to cover nymphs, emergers, and adult insects.

- Keep your flies organized according to type of insect and stage of life cycle. Keeping them in separate fly boxes will make it easier to locate the pattern you are looking for.

- Lessen your load by only taking those boxes that fit the stream and time of year you are fishing. For instance, you shouldn't need to take terrestrial patterns on an early spring outing.

RECOMMENDED ALL-PURPOSE FLIES

DRY FLIES
Adams, Blue-Winged Olive, Elk Hair Caddis, Grannom, Griffith's Gnat, Quill Gordon, Salmon Fly, Little Yellow Stonefly

WET FLIES/STREAMERS
Black Nose Dace, Muddler Minnow, Matuka, Woolly Bugger

ATTRACTORS
Humpy, Irresistable, Royal Wulff

EMERGERS
Emergent Sparkle Pupa, CDC Emerger, Soft Hackle

NYMPHS
Hare's Ear, Pheasant Tail

TERRESTRIALS
Grasshoppers, ants, beetles

8 READING THE WATER

Learning to read the water will increase your odds of success by allowing you to concentrate your efforts on the 10 percent of the water that holds 90 percent of the fish.

BASIC TROUT NEEDS

The key to reading the water is understanding that trout will hold in locations which supply them with one or all of these basic needs:

1. Food
2. Shelter from predators
3. Rest

LIES

In order to survive and grow, trout must eat more calories than they burn capturing food. Trout thus conserve energy by spending most of their time in specific locations called lies. Lies are places fish occupy in order to feed and/or rest—places, such as behind a rock or downed tree, that provide a break in the current or shelter from predators. A fish might occupy several different lies in a given day, depending on food availability and its desire to feed.

Although feeding lies can be different from sheltering lies, the most desirable lies provide food, shelter, and rest in one location. These combination lies will hold the most dominant trout, and will often be the most difficult places to fish. Once you learn these locations, return and you'll frequently find good-size trout.

Types of Lies

Edges

Edges—such as the edge of a faster current, the edge of a depth change, the edge of a shaded area, the edge of a weedbed or riverbank—hold fish because they concentrate drifting food, offer a break from the current, and are often near shelter.

Current Seams

Lines on the water indicate current seams, places where two currents converge. Trout will often hold on the slower side of the current seam, observing drifting food, which concentrates in the slower current.

An apparently featureless riffle with a slight depression can attract trout because it provides a horizontal current seam along the bottom.

Pools

Pools are areas of deeper water where the currents are slowest and the food tends to gather. Look for fish along the front and back edges of pools.

Eddies

Eddies are marked by a circular motion on the water's surface and occur on the sides of pools where the water runs against a bank and swirl back in the opposite direction, causing food to

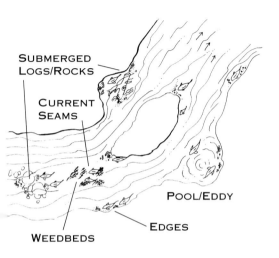

SUBMERGED LOGS/ROCKS

CURRENT SEAMS

POOL/EDDY

EDGES

WEEDBEDS

settle out of the current and encouraging feeding fish. Trout will face into the eddy current, not necessarily upstream, so approach them with stealth.

ALSO...

Look at bridges, logjams, submerged rocks or logs—anything that might provide a break from the current and a good place to hide.

Weedbeds, bottom depressions, areas of water that appear darker, overhanging vegetation, and riverbanks are also good places to look for trout.

Every time you spot a fish, file the scene away in your memory and try to understand what basic needs are being met in that location.

RISEFORMS

Reading the signs trout leave when feeding on or near the surface of the water will help you determine what types of insects they're eating and thus the appropriate flies to use.

SIMPLE RISE

Slow and deliberate, the simple rise leaves a small ring that often belies the true size of the trout. It indicates that the trout is feeding on small or spent insects on water's surface.

GULP RISE

This rise is made by a trout inhaling, often with mouth exposed, many flies from the surface, usu-

ally with an audible gulp. Air released through gills leaves a bubble on the water's surface.

BULGE RISE

The bulge rise is caused by a trout's back bulging or breaking the water. It indicates that the trout is

feeding on emerging insects just below surface. Use nymphs, emerger patterns.

SPLASHY, LEAPING RISE

This rise indicates aggressive pursuit, often triggered by an attractive but elusive food source, such as a skittering or emerging caddisfly.

SPOTTING FISH

Learning to spot fish will develop both your knowledge and enthusiasm. Moreover, casting to visible fish sharpens your concentration and stalking skills.

First, approach the river slowly and stealthfully, being careful to stay low and out of the trout's cone of vision. A trout looking upward sees through a cone that is a constant 97 degrees; the deeper the trout goes, the broader its view. Crouch low when approaching trout to stay out of their cone of vision.

8

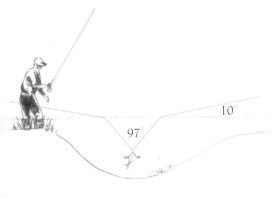

Angler in trout's cone of vision.

Direct your focus into the water and look at the bottom for any clue that might indicate a fish. Don't expect to see an entire fish—they're well camouflaged. Look for a waving tail fin, the white of an opening mouth, a puff of sediment, a brief flash from the side of a turning fish, a shadow on the bottom, movement, or any unusual disturbance of the water. A light spot on a dark bottom could be a spawning redd or feeding area dusted clean by fin movement.

Above all else, be patient. Fish in their element do not reveal their presence readily. Looking for fish requires time and care and stealth.

UNDERSTANDING WATER FLOW

To get a better idea of how water flows, take a three-foot piece of brightly colored yarn and tie it to the end of an old rod. Submerge the yarn at different depths, behind and in front of obstructions.

Observing the yarn will give you an idea of how water moves in various areas. Locations where the yarn swirls indicate the lack of a strong current and therefore possible holding spots.

You'll notice that there is a current seam running horizontally just above the river bottom. Here the yarn is not straightened by the current. The bottom of any river is likely to hold fish because the current is much slower and food is more readily available.

When surveying an unfamiliar river look for clues on the surface that could indicate holding locations. Pay attention to the ripple patterns on the surface; they indicate structure below. If visible, look at the bottom for depth and features. Turbulence created by the unevenness of the river bottom suggests nearby holding locations for trout.

FIGHTING GLARE

As mentioned in the gear chapter, polarized sunglasses reduce surface glare and allow you to see into the water more clearly. You can sometimes remove additional glare by tilting your head slightly to the side. But whenever possible keep the sun at your back or side and wear a hat with the brim darkened on the underside. When surveying an area of river look into shaded or darker areas first and allow time for your eyes to adjust, then look at the bright areas.

GENERAL TIPS

- When fishing a large river, mentally divide it into smaller rivers, eliminating from consideration the portion of the river that you cannot reach.

- Focus your efforts toward the primary locations where trout hold for shelter—along banks, shadows, deeper water, riffles, large rocks, and even bridges.

- Focus your efforts toward the primary locations where trout hold for food—along current seams, around vegetation, where waters of different temperatures meet, around rocks, and along the heads and tails of pools.

- Fish your chosen areas systematically to avoid spooking the fish nearest you. Start with short casts and gradually extend casting length as you work an area.

- Get as close as you can without spooking the fish.

- Always try to limit your false casts to avoid spooking fish. The fewer, the better.

- Try to present your flies with no drag first then add a little action if there are no takes

- Accurate casts should allow two to four feet of drag-free drift above the trout.

- Fishing upstream can be better because it puts you behind the trout's vision. Also, any disturbance you create will carry downstream and not affect upstream trout.

- If a particular spot is not yielding fish after a reasonable number of good presentations move on. The fishiest looking hole may not hold any fish. Moreover, exploring new water will add information to your memory banks, enhancing your scouting ability and angling success.

9 FIGHTING AND LANDING FISH

Fish are often lost because the angler doesn't know the proper amount of pressure to exert on the rod without breaking the tippet. Though such knowledge comes with onstream experience, a little prestream testing can perhaps save you a few lost fish. Simply hook your fly into a solid object and pull with the rod, gradually increasing tension until the tippet breaks. Do this a times until you get the feel for how much tension it takes to break the tippet. By contrast, give the line a quick jerk and it will break with much less force.

Note: Avoid practicing this with tippets testing six pounds or greater, because six-pound test can break some fly rods.

SETTING THE HOOK

Timing is the key to a good hook-set. You must react quickly enough to hook the fish before it spits out your artificial fly, but not so quickly that you yank the fly right out of the fish's mouth.

Reacting too soon is common in dry-fly fishing, where the excitement of seeing a fish rise to a fly can unsettle even the most steely veteran. You must remember to relax, and wait until the fly disappears before setting the hook.

The reverse is true of nymph fishing, where the strike occurs below the surface and is thus harder to detect. You can use a strike indicator, or you can take the slack out of your line and go by feel, waiting for the telltale twitch or tug. Either way, you must set the hook as soon as you see or feel evidence of a strike.

The motion required for setting the hook varies with the amount of slack that needs to be taken up. If the line is nearly straight, a gentle raise of the rod tip will tighten the line and set the hook. If there is slack in the line, a longer, quicker motion is needed. We recommend the "accordian" method: simply move your rod hand upward and to the right while simultaneously moving your line hand downward and to the left.

FISH ON!

FIGHTING FISH

Once the hook is set, try to get a feel for how big the fish is. If it's small enough and you can can bring it in quickly by stripping line with your line hand, do so. Never toy with a fish by extending a fight. The idea is to catch and release all fish as quickly as possible, which means using your tippet and tackle to its maximum capability. The longer the battle, the less the fish's chance for survival after release. This is especially true for smaller fish, which don't have the strength and stamina to endure much stress.

When fighting larger fish, reel in any loose line and play the fish from the reel, keeping the line tight, the pressure constant. If the fish runs with a strength great enough to break your tippet, let him take line from the reel, but work the line back as soon as the fish stops running, changes direction, or seems to tire. If the fish jumps, thrust the tip of your rod toward it to give it enough slack for its jump. Try to get downstream from the fish so the fish is fight-

ing both you and the current. Vary the direction of tension when possible, but be careful to avoid extreme bending of the rod.

Size your tippet accordingly for large fish. Light line for large fish can play the fish to exhaustion and cause it to die after release.

Most anglers instinctively keep the tension constant when fighting a fish, but there are times when giving slack is advantageous for the angler. For example, your reel is jammed and you're fighting the fish of a lifetime. Release the tension and the fish will stop fighting and usually find the nearest resting lie. This will give you time to untangle or make minor repairs.

LANDING AND RELEASING FISH

Always use a barbless hook, or pinch down existing barbs with a pair of needlenose pliers. This will allow you to release many fish without touching or lifting them from the water. If you must handle the fish, wet your hands first so that you don't damage its protective slime.

Hold it upside down and keep from touching its lateral line, and it may well stay quite docile.

Using a net will allow you to land big fish faster. Always lead the fish to the net; moving the net toward the fish will only spook it and thus lengthen the battle. Most fish big enough to use your reel's drag will need a period of revival before release. Hold the fish facing into the current, with one hand cupped gently under its tail and the other under its belly until it is ready to swim away. And remember, you should always try to release a fish without lifting it out of the water.

9

10 SPECIES

BROOK TROUT
(*Salvelinus fontinalis*)

The brook trout—also known as the eastern brook trout, speckled trout, square tail, or, more fondly, brookie—is actually a char and can be distinguished from its trout cousins by its light spots against a dark background (true trout have dark spots against a light background).

Perhaps the most brilliantly colored "trout," the brookie has wormlike markings on its back and dorsal fin, and cream and red spots bordered in

blue on its sides. Unique to the brook trout is a white front edge with black stripe on its reddish pectoral, ventral, and anal fins, and sometimes on its tail. Color varies with season and habitat. Lake or sea-run brook trout are light-colored or silver; river residents are more colorful; and fall spawners—especially the males—are more colorful still.

Brook trout typically range in size from 1 to 3 pounds, though fish over 14 pounds have been caught. Brook trout fare best in well-oxygenated water with temperatures between 55 and 65 degrees, and spawn in fall when water is 40 to 55 degrees.

NORTH AMERICAN DISTRIBUTION OF BROOK TROUT

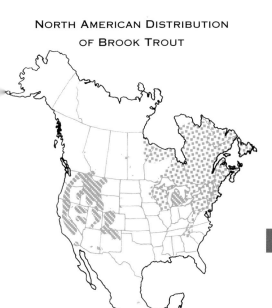

[::] NATIVE POPULATION OF BROOK TROUT

[▨] INTRODUCED POPULATION OF BROOK TROUT

10

BROWN TROUT
(*Salmo trutta*)

The brown trout is also known as the German brown or Loch Leven trout. Its olive green or brown upper body and dorsal and adipose fins display prominent dark spots surrounded by lighter halos. Midway down the sides are usually reddish haloed spots. Red on the adipose fin, though not always present, is a distinguishing characteristic. Its belly is usually yellow, though sometimes white or silver. Its tail and pectoral fins are rarely spotted. Resident river fish are intensely marked; lake and ocean-run browns are silver with faint, if any, markings, and are often confused with Atlantic salmon.

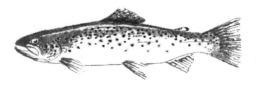

Browns thrive in waters with temperatures between 55 to 65 degrees and spawn from October through January. Brown trout commonly range between 1 to 6 pounds, with occasional fish over 35 pounds. Large older males will have a hooked lower jaw.

NORTH AMERICAN DISTRIBUTION
OF BROWN TROUT

10

▨ INTRODUCED POPULATION OF BROWN TROUT

RAINBOW TROUT
(*Oncorhynchus mykiss*)

The rainbow trout is also known as redband, redsides, or steelhead—the migratory form of rainbow, which attains a greater size. Rainbows usually display a pink stripe on their sides, but this may not be present in lake-resident fish. Coloration varies widely and is not always distinguishing. Compared to other trout, the head of a rainbow is short and blunt. Rainbows usually

range in size from 1 to 15 pounds, with occasional catches over 28 pounds. Of all trout, the rainbow is able to tolerate the widest range of water temperatures, but does best when the temperatures range from 45 to 65 degrees. Seventy-five degrees is the upper lethal limit. The rainbow is generally a spring spawner when water is 39 to 55 degrees (45 is considered optimum), and the coloration of both sexes intensifies during spawning. Large older males will have a hooked lower jaw.

NORTH AMERICAN DISTRIBUTION
OF RAINBOW TROUT

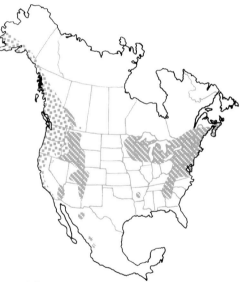

10

:: NATIVE POPULATION OF RAINBOW TROUT

▨ INTRODUCED POPULATION OF RAINBOW TROUT

CUTTHROAT TROUT
(*Oncorhynchus clarki*)

The cutthroat, though also known as the mountain, speckled, black spotted, or blueback trout, derives its common name from the red or orange bands on the underside of its lower jaw. The upper jaw extends beyond the back edge of the eye except in a few very large specimens. Its back is a dark olive green, its sides are olive to golden yellow, and its belly is usually silver. Its upper body displays dark spots that are more numerous near the tail. Mature fish

often exhibit a pink tint. Sea- or lake-run fish may be pale with faint coloration. There are many subspecies of cutthroat so coloration varies. Hybrids are common where other species have been introduced. The typical size range is 1 to 5 pounds, though fish up to 40 pounds have been caught. Cutthroats spawn in headwaters in the spring when water reaches 41 degrees. Fish drop back to lakes, larger rivers, or salt water after spawning.

NORTH AMERICAN DISTRIBUTION
OF CUTTHROAT TROUT

ANATOMY OF A TROUT

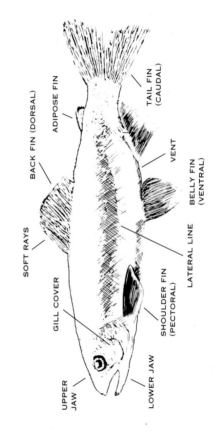

ADIPOSE FIN

BACK FIN (DORSAL)

TAIL FIN (CAUDAL)

VENT

BELLY FIN (VENTRAL)

LATERAL LINE

SOFT RAYS

GILL COVER

SHOULDER FIN (PECTORAL)

UPPER JAW

LOWER JAW

11 HATCHES

Learning the hatch schedules of the rivers you fish will help you determine which insects to expect at a given time, and thus which flies to choose. The following hatch charts offer only a general range of hatch activity for East/Midwest and Western regions. Exact dates will vary from stream to stream, and sometimes even within a stream. Changes or lack of changes in weather can also affect hatch activity, especially at the beginning or end of a hatch period. A bright sun and hot day may keep insects from emerging until later in the day, while a spring rain may get them moving early. Manmade changes to stream habitat, such as dams or impoundments, can also affect hatches.

The charts on the following pages identify insect types—mayflies (M), caddisflies (C), and stoneflies (S)—their Latin names, popular fly imitations, related hook sizes, and periods of activity.

Type	Latin Name	Name	Hook Size	Mar	Apr	May	June	July	Aug	Sep	Oct
M	Rithrogena morrisoni	Western Mach, Brown Black Quill	16, 14	■	■						
M	Baetis tricaudatus	Blue Wing Olive	18		■	■				■	■
M	Baetis bicaudatus	Blue Wing Olive	18, 16		■	■				■	■
M	Leptophlebia gravestella	Black Quill, Whirling Dun, Borchers Drake	14, 12			■	■				
M	Leptophlebia nebulosa	Black Quill, Whirling Dun, Borchers Drake	10–14			■	■				
M	Leptophlebia pacifica	Black Quill, Whirling Dun, Borchers Drake	8–12			■	■				
M	Callibaetis coloradensis nigritus	Speckly Wing Quill	16			■	■	■			
S	Pteronarcys californica	Western Salmon Fly	10, 6XL				■	■			
C	Hydropsyche occidentalis	Spotted Sedge	14				■	■	■		
M	Siphlonurus alternatus	Gray Drake	8–12				■	■			
M	Ephemerella inermis	Pale Morning Dun	18			■	■	■	■		
M	Hexegenia limbata	Michigan Caddis	6, 8, 4XL				■	■	■		
C	Rhyacophila coloradensis	Green (Gray) Sedge	14			■	■	■	■		

Type	Latin Name	Name	Hook Size	Mar	Apr	May	June	July	Aug	Sep	Oct
M	Baetis brunneicolor	Blue Wing Olive	18, 16								
M	Epeorus longimanus	Slate Gray Dun	14								
M	Siphlonurus occidentalis	Western Gray Drake	12 2XL								
M	Ephemerella flavilinea	Small Western Drake, Slate Wing Olive	16–12								
M	Rhithrogena hageni	Black Quill	14, 12								
M	Ephemera simulans	Brown Drake	12, 10 2XL								
M	Ephemerella grandis	Western Green Drake	12, 10 2XL								
M	Ephemerella infrequens	Pale Morning Dun	16								
M	Tricorythodes minutus	Trico, Tiny White Wing Black, Caenis	26, 24								
M	Caenis species	Caenis	26, 24								
M	Tricorythodes fallax	Trico, Tiny White Wing Black, Caenis	20								
M	Heptagenia simplicioides	Gray Drake	12, 14								
M	Isonychia velma	Leadwing Coachman, Dun Variant	8–12								

11

WESTERN HATCHES

Type	Latin Name	Name	Hook Size	Mar	Apr	May	June	July	Aug	Sep	Oct
M	Ephemerella doddsi	Western Green Drake	8,10								
M	Heptagenia elegantula	Western Red Quill, Gray Drake	16–12								
M	Paraleptophlebia debilus	Blue Quill, Blue Dun, Slate-wing Mahogany	16,18								
M	Cloeon ingens	Blue Wing Olive	14,16								
M	Epeorus albertae	Slate Cream Dun	16								
M	Pseudocloeon futile	Blue Wing Olive	26								
M	Rhithrogena undulata	Red Quill	16								
M	Pseudocloeon dubium	Blue Wing Olive	24,26								
M	Callibaetis coloradensis	Gray Quill	14,16								
M	Callibaetis nigritus	Gray Quill	12–16								
M	Baetis hageni	Tiny Blue Quill	22								
M	Ephoron album	White Fly	10,12								
M	Pseudocloeon edmundsi	Tiny Blue Wing Olive	22								
M	Paraleptophlebia bicornuta	Mahogany Dun	18–12								

EASTERN AND MIDWESTERN HATCHES

Type	Latin Name	Name	Hook	Jan	Feb	Mar	Apr	May	June	July	Aug	Sept	Oct
S	Allocapnia granulata or vivipara	Tiny Early Winter Black	18, 20	■	■								
S	Taeniopteryx Nivalis	Early Black	10–14		■	■							
S	Brachyptera fasciata	Early Brown	12, 14			■	■						
M	Baetis vagans	Blue Wing Olive	16–20				■	■				■	■
M	Epeorus pleuralis	Quill Gordon	10–14				■	■					
M	Baetis tricaudatus	Blue Wing Olive	14				■	■				■	■
C	Chimarra aterrima	Little Black Caddis	16, 18					■	■				
M	Baetis quebecensis	Blue Wing Olive	18						■	■			
M	Paraleptophlebia adoptiva	Blue Quill, Blue Dun, Little Mahogany	16, 18				■	■					
M	Ephemerella subvaria	Hendrickson, Red Quill	10–14				■	■					
M	Leptophlebia species	Black Quill, Whirling Dun	10–14					■					
M	Leptophlebia cupida	Black Quill, Borcher's Drake	12, 14						■	■			
S	Pteronarcys dorsata	Midwestern Salmon Fly	2–8						■	■			
C	Brachycentrus americanus	Grannom	14, 16				■	■					

11

EASTERN AND MIDWESTERN HATCHES

Type	Latin Name	Name	Hook	Jan	Feb	Mar	Apr	May	June	July	Aug	Sept	Oct
S	*Perlodidae*	Medium Brown Stonefly	8–14				■	■	■	■			
C	*Rhyacophilidae fenestra*	Green Rock Worm	10, 18				■	■	■	■	■	■	■
M	*Ephemerella rotunda*	Dark Hendrickson, Lt Hendrickson, Red Quill	12–16				■	■					
C	*Hydropsyche*	Net Building Caddis	14–20					■	■	■	■	■	■
M	*Baetis cingulatis*	Blue Wing Olive	20, 22				■	■	■	■	■	■	■
M	*Ephemerella invaria*	Sulphur, Pale Evening Dun, Hendrickson	14, 16					■	■				
M	*Stenonema vicarium*	March Brown, Brown Ginger Quill	8–12 XL					■	■	■			
S	*Alloperla caudata and imbecilla*	Little Yellow and Little Green Stonefly	14, 18						■	■	■		
C	*Nectopsyche*	White Miller	14, 16						■	■	■	■	
M	*Pseudocloeon carolina*	Blue Wing Olive	20, 22					■	■	■	■	■	
M	*Ephemera simulans*	Brown Drake	8–12					■	■				
M	*Ephemerella cornuta*	Blue Wing Olive	14, 16					■	■	■			
M	*Stenonema fuscum*	Gray Fox, Ginger Quill, Sand Drake	8–14					■	■	■	■		
M	*Ephemerella dorothea*	Little Sulphur, Sulphur, Pale Evening Dun	16, 18				■	■	■				

EASTERN AND MIDWESTERN HATCHES

Type	Latin Name	Name	Hook	Jan	Feb	Mar	Apr	May	June	July	Aug	Sept	Oct
M	Ephemera guttulata	Green Drake, Coffin Fly, Eastern Gray Drake	6,8, 8 XL										
M	Siphlonurus quebecensis	Gray Drake	8–12 XL										
M	Isonychia bicolor	Leadwing Coachman, Dun Variant	8–12										
M	Stenonema canadense	Light Cahill	10–14										
	Diptera (Midges)	Griffith's Gnat, Buzz Ball, Black Midge	20–28										
M	Isonychia sadleri	Leadwing Coachman, Mahogany Dun	8–12										
M	Ephemerella lata	Slate Wing Olive, Blue Wing Olive	14–18										
M	Epeorus vitreus	Sulphur, Pale Evening Dun	12,14										
M	Siphlonurus alternatus	Gray Drake	8–12										
T	Green Oak Worm	Caterpillar	8–12										
T	Terrestrials	Grasshoppers, ants, beetles, jasids	8–24										
M	Stenonema ithica	Light Cahill	10,12										
M	Ephemera varia	Yellow Drake, Yellow Dun, Cream Variant	8–10, 12 XL										
M	Hexagenia limbata	Giant Mayfly, Michigan Caddis	6, 8										

11

EASTERN AND MIDWESTERN HATCHES

Type	Latin Name	Name	Hook	Jan	Feb	Mar	Apr	May	June	July	Aug	Sept	Oct
M	*Ephemerella attenuata*	Blue Wing Olive	16, 18										
M	*Paraleptophlebia mollis*	Blue Quill, Dark Brown Spinner	14, 16										
M	*Baetis brunneicolor*	Blue Wing Olive	16, 18										
M	*Tricorythodes species*	Trico, Tiny White Wing Black, Caenis	24, 26										
M	*Pseudocloeon anoka*	Blue Wing Olive	20–24										
M	*Callibaetis species*	Gray Quill	14–18										
C	*Brachycercus species*	Grannom, Dark Brown Caddis	18–24										
M	*Ephemerella cornutella*	Blue Wing Olive	16, 18										
M	*Cloeon species*	Blue Wing Olive	20–26										
S	*Paragenetina media*	Big Golden Stonefly	6, 8										
M	*Paraleptophlebia debilis*	Blue Quill, Blue Dun, Slate Wing Mahogany	16, 18										
M	*Ephemerella depressa*	Blue Wing Olive	16, 18										
M	*Potomanthus distinctus*	Golden Drake, Yellow Drake, Cream Variant	8 2XL, 10										
M	*Tricorythodes stygiatus*	White Wing Black	24, 26										

EASTERN AND MIDWESTERN HATCHES

Type	Latin Name	Name	Hook	Jan	Feb	Mar	Apr	May	June	July	Aug	Sept	Oct
M	*Ephoron album*	White Fly	10–14								▓		
M	*Ephoron leukon*	White Fly	8–14								▓		

12 PURCHASING FLIES

WHEN PURCHASING FLIES:

Observe the hook. Test its sharpness (see test in chapter 2). The eye of the hook should be centered on the shank and should be tightly and neatly closed. Wet flies or streamers should be tied on heavy-wire hooks, dry flies on light-wire hooks. Look at the barb size. Barbless or small-barbed hooks are easier to remove.

Check fly proportions. Are they appropriate for that particular pattern?

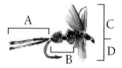

A Tail: full hook length
B Body: slightly more than ½ shank
C Wings: shank length
D Hackle Length: 1½ times gape

Examine dry-fly hackle for quality and proportion. The hackle barbs should be hard and smooth, not soft and webby.

The head of the fly should be neat, with no obstruction in or near the eye.

13 FLY FISHING THE INTERNET

You probably won't be bringing your portable computer with you onstream, but "fishing the net" has become quite popular these days. We have thus worked with the people at All Outdoors to provide much of this guide on-line at their World Wide Web site. You can contact us there with your comments:

- **ALL OUTDOORS AT**
  http://www.alloutdoors.com

With the number of fly fishing and outdoor re-lated sites well into the hundreds, fishing the net has never been easier nor more informative. Whether you're looking for travel information, guide services, or what's happening in you area or in an area you're heading to, you can find just about everything on the World Wide Web. Many sites provide chat rooms where you can discuss any number of issues or get asistance from other fly fishermen around the world.

To get a really long list of fly fishing sites you can search for "fly fishing" using any of the popu-lar search engines currently available.

13

RECOMMENDED READING

Borger, Gary. *Nymphing*. Stackpole Books, 1979.

Borger, Gary. *Naturals: A Guide to Food Organisms of the Trout*. Stackpole Books, 1980.

Brooks, Charles. *The Trout and the Stream*. Crown Publishers, 1974.

Brooks, Charles. *Nymph Fishing for Larger Trout*. Crown Publishers, 1976.

Caucci, Al and Bob Nastasi. *Hatches II*. Lyons & Burford, Publishers, 1990.

Combs, Trey. *Steelhead Fly Fishing*. Lyons & Burford, Publishers, 1991.

Harvey, George W. *Techniques of Trout Fishing and Fly Tying*. Lyons & Burford, Publishers, 1990.

Humphreys, Joe. *Joe Humphrey's Trout Tactics, Updated and Expanded*. Stackpole Books, 1993.

Jaworowski, Ed. *The Cast*. Stackpole Books, 1991.

Lafontaine, Gary. *Caddisflies*. Nick Lyons Books, 1981.

Lafontaine, Gary. *The Dry Fly*. Greycliff Press 1990.

Lafontaine, Gary. *Trout Flies Proven Patterns*. Greycliff Press 1993.

Koch, Ed. *Fishing the Midge*. Stackpole Books, 1988.

Koch, Ed. *Terrestrial Fishing.* Stackpole Books, 1990.

Kreh, Lefty. *Longer Fly Casting.* Lyons & Burford, Publishers, 1991.

Kreh, Lefty. *Modern Fly Casting Method.* Odysseus Editions, Inc., 1991.

Marinaro, Vincent C. *A Modern Dry Fly Code.* G. P. Putnam's Sons, 1950; Crown Publishers Inc., 1970.

McClane, A. J. *The Practical Fly Fisherman.* Prentice-Hall, 1975.

Nemes, Sylvester. *The Soft Hackle Fly.* The Chatham Press, 1975.

Proper, Datus. *What the Trout Said.* Nick Lyons Books, 1989.

Richards, Bruce. *Modern Fly Lines.* Odysseus Editions, Inc., 1994.

Sosin, Mark and Lefty Kreh. *Fishing the Flats.* Lyons & Burford, Publishers, 1983.

Sosin, Mark and Lefty Kreh. *Practical Fishing Knots II.* Lyons & Burford, Publishers, 1991.

Swisher, Doug and Carl Richards. *Selective Trout.* Crown Publishers Inc., 1971.

Swisher, Doug and Carl Richards. *Emergers.* Lyons & Burford, Publishers, 1991.

Whitlock, Dave. *Guide to Aquatic Trout Foods.* Nick Lyons Books, 1982.

Wulff, Lee. *Trout on a Fly.* Lyons & Burford, Publishers, 1986.

GLOSSARY

aquatic insects Insects that begin life in the water. Trout prey both on the immature insects living underwater and the adults emerging from the water or returning to lay eggs.

arbor The axle of a fly reel, on which the spool revolves.

attractor An artificial fly that will excite a fish to strike even though it does not resemble any specific natural food.

backing Strong, braided line running between the reel and the fly line, which permits a fish to make long runs.

barb The rear-facing piece of metal just behind the point of the hook, which helps prevent the hook from coming loose. The barb can be flattened with a pair of pliers, allowing you to release fish more easily.

caddisfly Any one of a group of aquatic insects that undergo a complete metamorphosis, progressiving from egg to larva to pupa to adult. Caddisflies provide an important food source for trout.

current seam A place where two water currents converge.

dead drift Letting the fly drift downstream affected only by the current.

direct-drive A type of reel with the handle directly connected to the spool; one turn of the handle results in one turn of the spool.

double taper Fly line that is thinner on both ends and thicker in the middle. It can be reversed when one end wears out, thereby doubling the life of the line.

drag (fly) Unnatural movement of a fly caused by either wind or water currents acting against the leader, drag will inhibit a fish from striking.

dropper An extra fly tied to another fly or to the leader, a dropper can increase your chances of getting a strike.

dry fly An artificial fly designed to ride on or just at the water's surface.

dun A newly-emerged adult mayfly, which floats on the current until its wings are dry. It resembles a tiny sailboat, and is most vulnerable to trout.

eddy A current of water on the edge of a stream where the water hits the bank and swirls in the opposite direction of the main current.

edges Areas that hold fish because they concentrate drifting food, offer a break from the current, or are near shelter (For example, the edge of a faster current, the edge of a depth change, or the edge of a shaded area).

emerger An aquatic insect midway through its development, either a pupae or a nymph, as it is making its way to the water's surface.

entomology The study of insects.

false cast A false cast is simply a regular cast done without allowing the fly to land. Used to practice casting or to dry a damp fly.

flotant A susbtance applied to flies, leaders, and fly line to keep them afloat.

hackle Feathers used in artificial flies, usually taken from the back or neck of a chicken or game bird.

hatch Time when large numbers of aquatic insects shed pupal cases and rise to the water's surface to emerge as adults; actual mass of emerging insects.

hauling Pulling the fly line with the line hand during the acceleration stroke, used to add line speed and distance to a cast.

knotless leader A single strand of tapered monofilament connecting the fly line to the fly.

larva In aquatic insects such as caddisflies and midges, the developmental stage between egg and pupa.

lateral line (fish's) Sensory cells that run down both sides of a fish, used to warn the fish of predators and to help it seek out prey.

leader Section of monfilament attached to the fly line, is harder for fish to detect and allows proper fly presentation.

lies Places fish occupy in the stream in order to rest or feed, where there is a break in the current or shelter from predators.

loop The shape of the fly line before it unrolls completely during the backcast and forward cast. Also, a type of connection on lines and leaders.

loop-to-loop The connection of two loops to join the leader to the fly line, or to attach tippets.

mayfly Any one of a group of aquatic insects that are a food source for freshwater fish.

mending Flipping the the rod tip upstream in a semicircular motion to adjust the line and leader to allow a drag-free drift.

midge Any of several tiny aquatic insects that are prey to freshwater fish.

monofilament Single-strand nylon line of varying diameter, used to create leaders and tippets.

nymph The stage of an aquatic insect's life between hatching from its egg and emerging from the water as an adult.

pickup The beginning of an overhead cast, entails getting the fly off the water to start the backcast.

polarized lenses Sunglass lenses that reduce the glare from the water, enabling a better view under the surface.

pound test Pound test indicates how strong a fishing line is, defined by how much weight it can hold before breaking.

presentation Placing the fly on the water as the final part of a cast. Also, how the angler moves the fly in the water to attract fish.

pupa In the midge or caddisfly, the developmental stage between larvae and adult.

rise A fish coming to the water's surface to take an insect.

rod action Action refers to how rigid a fishing rod is, and indicates where it bends. A fast-action rod bends only near the tip when casting; a slow-action rod flexes its entire length.

roll cast Used when wind or obstructions prevent a normal backcast. Tilt the rod back until the line is behind the shoulder, then make a normal forward cast.

running line A section of the fly line from the front tapered section to the backing connection.

shoot To allow line to be pulled through the rod guides by the momentum of the cast.

shooting head A section of line attached to the front of the fly line to allow a longer cast.

slack A lack of tension in the line, enabling drag-free presentation of a fly.

spinner The last stage in the lifecycle of a may-fly, during which mating occurs, eggs are deposited, and the insects float dead or dying on the water's surface.

spool The part of the reel that holds the line.

standing part The main part of the line left connected to a knot.

stonefly An aquatic insect with a two-stage lifecyle, progressing directly from nypmh to adult, and a consistently available food source for fish.

streamer An artificial fly generally used to immitate a fish.

strike A fish biting a fisherman's fly. Also, setting the hook into a fish.

strike indicator A brightly-colored buoyant material attached to the leader, alerting the fisher that a fish has taken a fly under the water.

strip To pull line with your line hand, either from the the reel or back through the rod guides to recover a fly.

stripping guide The first guide ring at the butt of the rod.

structure Changes in the shape of the stream bottom, or objects such as rock or logs, which provide protection, rest, or feeding lies for fish.

tag end The section of line from the knot to the end of the line, usually trimmed after the knot is seated.

taper The gradual decrease in the width of a line, leader, or rod.

terrestrials Non-aquatic insects such a grasshoppers, beetles, or ants, which become prey for fish when they fall into the water, or the artificial flies designed to imitate them.

tippet The part of the leader attached to the fly.

tip-top The last guide ring at the tip of the rod.

waders Waterproof legwear, either boot or stockingfoot, used in fishing.

wading shoes Shoes worn over stockingfoot waders, generally with cleated or felt soles.

weight-forward taper Fishing line that is thin on one end, tapers to a thick section, then tapers back down to a thin running line.

wet fly An artificial fly designed to sink under the water to immitate an aquatic insect or fish.

wind knot A knot in the line or leader resulting from a casting flaw.

INDEX